R Programming Unlocked: Easy Learning

Md. Sifat Hossain

Dr. Provash Kumar Karmokar

Welcome to "*R Programming Unlocked: Easy Learning*," your comprehensive guide to mastering the R programming language. This book is designed to take you from a beginner to an advanced user, equipping you with the skills needed to tackle a wide range of statistical and data analysis tasks.

R has emerged as a powerful tool in the field of data science due to its flexibility, extensive package ecosystem, and strong community support. Whether you're a student, a researcher, or a professional data analyst, understanding R will open doors to new possibilities in data manipulation, visualization, and advanced statistical modeling.

In this book, you will find a structured approach to learning R, starting with the basics and progressively moving towards more complex topics. We begin with an introduction to R and its origins, followed by detailed instructions on installing R and RStudio, the preferred integrated development environment (IDE) for R. You'll learn about the various components of RStudio and how they can enhance your coding experience.

The book covers essential R programming concepts, including operators, variable naming conventions, and data objects such as vectors, matrices, data frames, and lists. We also delve into statistical operations, conditional structures, and looping mechanisms to help you perform robust data analyses. Additionally, you'll explore advanced topics like matrix operations, string handling, and creating user-defined functions.

To facilitate practical learning, we have included sections on reading and writing data files, working with strings, and implementing measures of central tendency and dispersion. Each section of this book is designed to build on the previous ones, ensuring a smooth learning curve.

Furthermore, this book emphasizes the importance of a questioning mindset in mastering advanced R programming. By encouraging curiosity and providing guidelines for continuous improvement, we aim to help you develop a deep and intuitive understanding of R.

For those looking to push their R skills even further, we recommend leveraging AI tools such as ChatGPT, Gemini, PoeClaude, and SocraAI. These tools can provide personalized assistance, generate code snippets, debug issues, and offer advanced insights, making your learning journey more efficient and enjoyable.

We would like to express our gratitude to the R community for their continuous contributions and support, which have made R a versatile and powerful tool for data analysis. Special thanks to our reviewers and beta readers for their invaluable feedback, and to our families and friends for their unwavering support.

We hope that this book will serve as a valuable resource in your journey to mastering R programming. Happy coding!

Late Professor Dr. Md. Janahur Rahman

The Authors

Md. Sifat Hossain
MPhil Research Fellow
Department of Statistics
University of Rajshahi
Rajshahi-6205

Dr. Provash Kumar Karmokar
Professor
Department of Statistics,
University of Rajshahi
Rajshahi-6205

Contacts

+8801863504629 (WhatsApp, Telegram, Viber)
sifat.stat@gmail.com
https://www.facebook.com/msh.stat
https://www.linkedin.com/in/sifatstat
https://orcid.org/0009-0000-7265-5143
https://www.researchgate.net/profile/Md-Hossain-1441

Table of Contents

1 Introduction

In data-driven decision-making, R has emerged as a powerful tool for statisticians, data scientists, researchers, and analysts. With its open-source nature and an ever-expanding ecosystem of packages, R has become the go-to programming language for those seeking to unlock the hidden insights within data.

Whether you're a novice embarking on your data analysis journey or an experienced statistician looking to expand your skill set, this book is designed to be your comprehensive companion. We will take you on a journey through the world of R, demystifying its complexities, and showing you how to harness its potential for practical, real-world data analysis.

1.1 Why R

R is more than just a programming language; it's a community-driven platform that thrives on collaboration and innovation. Its versatility makes it suitable for a wide range of tasks, from basic statistical analysis to advanced machine learning and data visualization. But why should you choose R for your data analysis needs?

1. **Open Source:** R is open-source, which means it's freely available to anyone. You can download, use, and modify it without incurring any licensing costs [1]–[3].

2. **Rich Ecosystem:** R boasts an extensive library of packages created by the R community. These packages cover everything from data manipulation and visualization to specialized statistical techniques.

3. **Powerful Graphics:** R is renowned for its data visualization capabilities. With libraries like 'ggplot2', you can create stunning and informative data visualizations.

4. **Reproducibility:** R makes it easy to create reproducible analyses. You can document your code, ensuring that others can understand and replicate your work.

5. **Statistical Prowess:** R was built with statistics in mind. It excels at traditional statistical analysis, making it an ideal choice for statisticians and researchers.

1.2   What You'll Find in This Book

In this book, we've structured the content to cater to learners at various stages of their R and statistical journey. Here's a brief overview of what you can expect:

1. Discover the significance of R in data analysis and statistics, highlighting its flexibility and the thriving community behind it.

2. Navigate the installation process for R and uncover the advantages of using RStudio, a leading IDE.

3. Explore the essentials of RStudio, the central hub for your R projects, while introducing essential packages and libraries.

4. Equip yourself with the skills to access help and manuals within R, and learn about valuable online resources to enhance your learning experience.

5. Gain a solid foundation in project organization, covering setting your working directory, installing packages, and establishing best practices.

6. Understand the fundamental building blocks of R, including arithmetic, assignment, comparison, and logical operators, as well as the powerful pipe operator (%>%).

7. Dive into basic statistical operations in R, encompassing arithmetic, assignment, comparison, and logical operations.

8. Master the art of variable naming in R, exploring naming rules, conventions, and best practices for code clarity and efficiency.

9. Uncover the core data manipulation techniques, including R data objects, matrix operations, data frame operations, and statistical operations.

10. Learn to implement conditional structures in R to control program flow and make dynamic decisions.

11. Harness the power of loops for task automation, exploring various loop types and practical applications.

12. Embrace the world of functions in R, including built-in, user-defined, recursive, and function calls.

13. Dive into the realm of strings, essential for data cleaning, with a focus on string operations like splitting, space removal, and pattern matching.

14. Master the art of reading and writing data files in R, preparing your data for analysis effectively.

15. Explore measures of central tendency, including arithmetic mean (AM), harmonic mean (HM), geometric mean (GM), mode, and median, all within the R environment.

16. Grasp measures of dispersion, covering both absolute and relative measures, to evaluate data variability effectively.

By the time you reach the end of this book, you'll have the confidence and skills to tackle data analysis challenges head-on. You'll be able to perform meaningful analyses, and make data-driven decisions.

So, let's embark on this exciting journey together. Let's unlock the potential of R and empower you to become a proficient data analyst and statistician. Get ready to dive into the world of programming, armed with the knowledge and skills you'll acquire in the pages that follow.

Let's begin our adventure with R!

1.3 The Birth of R in New Zealand

Before we delve into the intricacies of R and its practical applications, it's worth taking a moment to explore the origins of this remarkable programming language.

R was conceived in the land of the Kiwis, New Zealand, by Ross Ihaka and Robert Gentleman in the early 1990s. Ross Ihaka [4], a statistician at the University of Auckland, and Robert Gentleman, a computer scientist, joined forces to create a tool that would revolutionize the world of statistical computing.

Their collaboration resulted in the birth of R, a language and environment that combined statistical expertise with the power of programming. This innovation would go on to transform the way data analysis and statistical modeling are conducted worldwide.

R was designed with a fundamental principle in mind: to be open-source and freely accessible to anyone with an interest in data analysis and statistics. This openness paved the way for a vibrant and collaborative community of users and developers, contributing to the continuous growth and improvement of the R ecosystem.

As we journey through the pages of this book, we'll be building upon the foundation laid by Ihaka and Gentleman. We'll explore how R has evolved into a versatile tool for data analysis and statistics, enabling professionals and enthusiasts alike to extract meaningful insights from data.

2   Installing R

Installing R and RStudio is a straightforward process, and I'll provide you with step-by-step instructions for both.

1. **Download R:** Visit the Comprehensive R Archive Network (CRAN) website [5], where you can download the R installation package appropriate for

your operating system: CRAN website: [https://cran.r-project.org/mirrors.html].

2. **Select a CRAN Mirror:** Choose a CRAN mirror site near your location. This will be where the R installation package is downloaded from. Pick a mirror that's geographically close to you for faster downloads.

3. **Download R:** Click on the link corresponding to your operating system (Windows, macOS, or Linux) to download the R installation package. Follow the on-screen instructions to save the file to your computer.

4. **Install R:**

   a. **For Windows:** Double-click the downloaded .exe file and follow the installation prompts.

   b. **For macOS:** Double-click the downloaded .pkg file and follow the installation prompts.

   c. **For Linux:** Follow the instructions specific to your distribution. You can often use your package manager to install R (e.g., 'sudo apt-get install r-base' on Ubuntu).

5. **Verify Installation:** To confirm that R was installed successfully, open a command prompt or

terminal and type 'R' to launch the R console. You should see the R prompt ('>'), indicating that R is ready for use.

2.1   Installing RStudio

1. **Download RStudio:** Visit the RStudio download page to get the RStudio installation package: RStudio download page: [https://www.rstudio.com/products/rstudio/download/].

2. **Select RStudio Desktop:** On the download page, find and select "RStudio Desktop" (the free and open-source version). There is also a paid version called RStudio Server for different use cases.

3. **Choose Your RStudio Version:** Depending on your operating system (Windows, macOS, or Linux), select the appropriate version of RStudio for download.

4. **Download RStudio:** Click on the download link to save the RStudio installation package to your computer.

   a. **Install RStudio:** For Windows: Double-click the downloaded .exe file and follow the installation prompts. RStudio will automatically detect your R installation.

b. **For macOS:** Double-click the downloaded .dmg file and drag the RStudio application to your Applications folder.

c. **For Linux:** Follow the instructions specific to your distribution for installation.

5. **Launch RStudio:** Once installed, you can launch RStudio from your applications menu or by double-clicking its icon. RStudio will automatically integrate with your installed R version.

6. **Verify Installation:** When RStudio starts, you should see a clean and organized interface with a script editor, console, and other tools. This confirms that RStudio was installed successfully.

You're now ready to start using R and RStudio for your data analysis and statistical tasks. Enjoy your journey with these powerful tools!

2.2 Why RStudio is Better

RStudio stands out as the preferred environment for working with R due to its feature-rich and user-friendly interface designed explicitly for data analysis and programming tasks. Unlike the basic R console, RStudio offers an IDE that streamlines the entire workflow. It boasts essential features such as code highlighting, auto-completion, interactive graphics, native support for R Markdown, and Shiny app development tools. These capabilities empower users to create dynamic reports, interactive web applications, and documents seamlessly. Additionally, RStudio simplifies project management, integrates version control, and provides advanced error handling and debugging tools, enhancing productivity and code quality. The active RStudio community and its cross-platform compatibility further contribute to its reputation as the go-to choose for individuals and teams engaged in data-driven research and analysis.

Table 1 Comparisons between R and RStudio

Feature	R	RStudio
Definition	A programming language for statistical computing and graphics.	A complete IDE for R.
Purpose	Designed for data analysis, statistical modeling, and data visualization.	Designed to enhance the user experience when working with R.

Feature	R	RStudio
Development	Developed by the R Development Core Team and the R community.	Developed by RStudio, Inc., an independent company.
Open Source	Yes, R is open-source and freely available.	RStudio offers both open-source (free) and commercial versions.
Functionality	Provides a wide range of statistical functions and libraries.	Offers code editing, debugging, package management, and more.
Console	Has a basic command-line console.	Provides an enhanced R console with features like syntax highlighting, code completion, and history.
Script Editor	Typically used with a separate text editor.	Includes a built-in script editor with code highlighting, debugging tools, and version control integration.
Package Management	Packages can be installed and	Provides a package manager for easier

Feature	R	RStudio
	loaded from within R.	package installation and management.
Graphics	Offers base graphics and additional packages for advanced data visualization.	Enhances graphics with interactive plots and charting features.
Data Manipulatio n	Requires additional libraries like dplyr and tidyr for efficient data manipulation.	Integrates with packages like dplyr and tidyr for streamlined data cleaning and transformation.
Debugging	Offers basic debugging tools like browser() and traceback().	Provides an integrated debugging environment with breakpoints, variable inspection, and error messages.
Workspace	Stores data and objects in a separate environment.	Manages your workspace with easy access to data, plots, and objects.
Project Management	Lacks built-in project	Facilitates project organization with

Feature	R	RStudio
	management features.	dedicated project folders, version control, and management tools.
Customization	Highly customizable through R scripts and packages.	Offers customization options through themes, key bindings, and extensions.
Community Support	Relies on the R community and online forums for support.	Offers its own community forum and support resources, in addition to R resources.
Cross-Platform	Available on Windows, macOS, and Linux.	Available on Windows, macOS, and Linux, ensuring cross-platform compatibility.
Code Prediction	Basic code prediction capabilities.	Advanced code prediction and autocompletion features, enhancing coding efficiency.

Feature	R	RStudio
Color	Limited syntax highlighting for code readability.	Extensive syntax highlighting for improved code readability and differentiation.
Error Messages	Standard error messages.	Enhanced error messages with interactive debugging and traceback information.
Installation Guide	Manual download and installation from CRAN.	Simplified installation process with downloadable installer packages.
Indentation Facilities	Manual indentation.	Automatic code indentation and formatting for cleaner code.
R Markdown	Not natively supported in base R.	Offers native support for creating interactive documents, reports, and presentations using R Markdown.

Feature	R	RStudio
Shiny App Facilities	Not natively supported in base R.	Provides a dedicated Shiny application development environment for creating interactive web apps directly from RStudio.

3   Getting Started with RStudio

RStudio is a powerful IDE designed for R programming. Understanding the layout and components of RStudio is essential for efficient coding and data analysis. In this section, we'll explore the various elements of RStudio and how they contribute to your workflow.

3.1   Introduction to RStudio

3.1.1   Script File Editor

The script file editor is your primary workspace in RStudio. It's where you write, edit, and save your R code. You can create a new script file by navigating to File > New File > R Script or by using the keyboard shortcut Ctrl+Shift+N (Windows/Linux) or Command+Shift+N (macOS). This is where you'll write your R code, including data analysis, functions, and visualizations.

3.1.2   Console

The console is an interactive pane in RStudio where you can enter and run R commands line by line. It's a great place to experiment with code or quickly test a function. You can open the console by clicking on the "Console" tab located in the bottom left corner of RStudio or by using the keyboard shortcut Ctrl+2 (Windows/Linux) or Command+2 (macOS).

3.1.3   Environment Pane

The Environment pane, typically situated in the top right corner of RStudio, provides vital information about your current R environment. Here, you can inspect the variables, datasets, and objects you're working with. Understanding your environment is crucial for tracking and managing your data.

3.1.4   Files/Plots/Packages/Help Pane

In the bottom right corner, RStudio offers multiple tabs: "Files," "Plots," "Packages," and "Help."

- **Files**: The "Files" tab allows you to navigate and manage the files and directories in your project.

- **Plots**: The "Plots" tab displays graphical plots when you create them.

- **Packages**: The "Packages" tab provides information about the R packages currently loaded in your session.

- **Help**: The "Help" tab displays R documentation, making it easy to access information about R functions and packages.

3.1.5 Viewer Pane

The Viewer pane is used for rendering HTML-based content, including Shiny applications and HTML help files. It's a handy feature for interactive data visualization and exploring HTML-based reports.

3.1.6 Version Control Integration

RStudio integrates seamlessly with version control systems like Git. You can manage version control operations directly from the IDE, making it easier to track changes and collaborate with others on your projects.

3.1.7 Toolbar

At the top of RStudio, you'll find a toolbar that provides quick access to common operations such as saving scripts, running code, and managing version control. The toolbar streamlines your workflow and saves you time.

3.1.8 Menus

RStudio offers standard menus including "File," "Edit," "View," "Code," "Build," "Session," and "Help." These menus provide access to a wide range of functions and options, making it easy to customize your IDE experience.

3.1.9 Source & Terminal Tabs

RStudio allows you to work on multiple script files simultaneously. You can switch between open script files using the "Source" tab. If you need to open a terminal for command-line operations, you can do so via the "Terminal" tab.

In the upcoming sections, we'll delve deeper into each of these components, exploring how to write and run R code, manage data, create visualizations, and much more.

3.2 Packages & Libraries in R

In R, "packages" and "libraries" are often used interchangeably. However, they refer to the same concept - collections of functions, datasets, and documentation that extend the capabilities of the R programming language. These packages or libraries can be created by developers and the R community to provide specialized tools and functions for various tasks.

- **Packages**: A "package" is a set of functions, datasets, and documentation bundled together to perform specific tasks. Packages are like toolboxes that you can use to extend R's base functionality. You can think of them as add-ons to R, each designed to address a particular set of needs.

- **Library**: To use a package in R, you typically need to load it into your R session. The process of loading a package is sometimes referred to as "attaching" or "importing" a library. When you load a library, you make its functions and datasets available for use in your current R session.

3.2.1 Common Libraries

Here are some common and highly useful libraries for statistics in R:

1. **base**: The base package contains the fundamental functions and datasets that come with R. It is loaded automatically when you start R and includes basic statistical functions like mean, median, variance, and standard deviation.

2. **stats**: The stats package is a part of the R base package and provides a wide range of statistical functions and tests, including t-tests, regression models, ANOVA, and more.

3. **dplyr**: The dplyr package is a powerful library for data manipulation. It provides functions like filter, select, mutate, and summarize to efficiently clean and manipulate data.

4. **ggplot2**: The ggplot2 package is a popular choice for data visualization. It enables you to create elegant and informative graphs and plots with a high degree of customization.

5. **lubridate**: The lubridate package is used for handling date and time data. It makes it easier to work with date objects and perform time-based calculations.

6. **broom**: The broom package helps convert the results of statistical models (e.g., regression models) into tidy data frames, making it easier to work with and visualize model output.

7. **car**: The car package provides various functions for regression diagnostics and model validation. It's particularly useful when working with regression models.

8. **tidyr**: The tidyr package, part of the "tidyverse," is used for reshaping and tidying data. It provides functions like gather and spread to make data in long or wide format.

9. **stringr**: The stringr package is helpful for string manipulation and regular expressions, which can be crucial when dealing with text data in statistics.

10. **MASS**: The MASS package contains various functions and datasets for multivariate analysis, including linear and non-linear modeling.

11. **survival**: The survival package is used for survival analysis, including Kaplan-Meier survival curves and Cox proportional hazards models.

These libraries, among many others, cover a wide range of statistical and data analysis needs. When working on statistical projects in R, you can load these libraries to access their functions and datasets, greatly expanding the capabilities of R for statistical analysis and data manipulation.

4   Getting Help & Accessing Manuals

R is a rich and versatile programming language, and learning it can be a rewarding experience. One of the key aspects that make R user-friendly is the abundance of resources available for learning, troubleshooting, and expanding your knowledge. In this section, we'll explore how to access help and manuals in R, empowering you to harness the full potential of this powerful language.

4.1 Accessing Help in R

4.1.1 Using the help() Function

R provides a built-in help() function that allows you to access documentation for functions, packages, and topics. To access help for a specific function, simply type:

help(mean)

This command will open a help page in the R console, providing you with detailed information on the mean function, its parameters, and usage.

4.1.2 Shortcut: ? Prefix

A convenient shortcut is to use the ? prefix before a function or topic. For example, to access the help page for the mean function, you can use:

?mean

This will display the same documentation as the help() function.

4.2 Package Manuals

Many R packages come with extensive documentation. To access the manual for a specific package, you can use the help.start() function, which opens the package index. For example:

help.start()

This will open a web page with links to package manuals. You can browse through the manuals to learn more about the functions and capabilities of the packages you're using.

4.3 Online Resources

4.3.1 CRAN Package Manuals

The CRAN hosts comprehensive manuals for many packages. You can access these manuals on the CRAN website, typically in PDF format. These manuals offer in-depth information on package usage and functionality.

4.3.2 Online Platforms for Discussion

R has a vibrant and supportive online community. You can join discussions, ask questions, and share your knowledge on platforms like:

- **Stack Overflow**: A popular Q&A platform where you can find answers to your R-related questions and contribute by helping others.

- **RStudio Community**: RStudio hosts an active community where you can discuss R-related topics, seek advice, and collaborate with fellow R users.

- **GitHub**: Many R packages and projects are hosted on GitHub, making it a great place to explore code, report issues, and collaborate with developers.

- **R Bloggers**: A community of R bloggers who share their insights, code, and experiences.

R is ready to help you learn and use its vast capabilities. With a wealth of examples and comprehensive manuals at your fingertips, you'll find the resources you need to become proficient in R and make the most of this versatile language. In the following sections, we'll dive into practical examples and in-depth tutorials to enhance your understanding and proficiency in R.

5   Project Organization in R

Setting the working directory and package installation are fundamental tasks in R that contribute to efficient project organization. In this section, we will cover both aspects, and we'll also explore how to install packages from CRAN, GitHub, and from local files, including offline installations.

5.1   Working Directory & Environment

The working directory is a pivotal concept in R, determining the default location for file operations. Properly setting the working directory enhances your project's organization and accessibility.

5.1.1   Manual Working Directory Setup

You can manually set the working directory using the setwd() function:

```r
# Manually set the working directory to your project
folder
setwd("C:/Your/Project/Directory")
getwd()


# "C:/Your/Project/Directory"
```

However, manual setup can become cumbersome, especially when managing multiple projects.

5.1.2   Automating Working Directory Setup

To automate working directory setup, consider the following techniques:

RStudio Projects: RStudio provides a seamless way to manage working directories with "Projects." When you create an RStudio Project, the working directory is automatically set to the project's location. Here's how to create a project:

1.   Open RStudio.

2.   Go to "File" > "New Project."

3.   Choose the project type (New Directory, Existing Directory, or Version Control).

4.   Specify the project's location.

5.   Click "Create Project."

With this approach, opening an R file within the project automatically sets the working directory to the project's location.

Script Header Comments: Alternatively, you can include a comment at the top of your R script to set the working directory:

```r
# Set the working directory to the location of this R script
setwd(dirname(rstudioapi::getActiveDocumentContext()$path))
```

This comment dynamically adjusts the working directory to match the location of the currently opened R script.

5.1.3   Clearing Environment

To remove all the previously saved objects in the R system we need to run the following code. For avoiding ambiguity, we must clear the environment for a new start.

```r
rm(list = ls())
```

5.2   Package Installation

Packages extend R's capabilities by providing additional functions and data sets. Installing packages is essential for leveraging a wide range of tools for data analysis and visualization.

5.2.1   Installing Packages from CRAN

You can install packages from the CRAN using the install.packages() function:

```r
# Install the "dplyr" package from CRAN
install.packages("dplyr")
```

This command installs the "dplyr" package from the official CRAN repository.

5.2.2   Offline Package Installation

In some scenarios, you may need to install packages offline, such as when working on a computer with restricted internet access. You can download the package source files from CRAN or GitHub, transfer them to the offline machine, and install them from local files. Here's how:

1.   Download the package source files (usually in the form of a .tar.gz or .zip file) from CRAN or GitHub.

2. Transfer the downloaded files to the offline machine.

3. Install the package using the local file path:

```r
# Install the package from a local file
install.packages("path/to/package.tar.gz", repos = NULL, type = "source")
```

Replace "path/to/package.tar.gz" with the actual file path.

In the following sections, we will delve into additional data management and project organization techniques to further optimize your workflow in R.

6   Operators in R

In the realm of data analysis and statistical computing, mastering the use of operators is fundamental. Operators in R are symbols or special characters that enable you to perform various operations on data, variables, and objects. Whether you're performing basic arithmetic calculations or complex data transformations, understanding and utilizing operators efficiently is essential for becoming proficient in R.

6.1   Arithmetic Operator

Let's begin with the arithmetic operators, the building blocks of mathematical operations in R:

1. **Addition (+):** The addition operator, denoted by '+', combines two numbers to produce their sum. For example, '3 + 5' yields '8'.

2. **Subtraction (-):** Subtraction is performed using the '-' operator. It subtracts the right operand from the left operand. For instance, '10 - 4' results in '6'.

3. **Multiplication (*):** To multiply numbers, use the '*' operator. For example, '2 * 6' equals '12'.

4. **Division (/):** Division is achieved with the '/' operator. For example, '15 / 3' gives '5'.

5. **Modulus (%):** The modulus operator '%' returns the remainder when the left operand is divided by the right operand. For example, '17 % 4' equals '1'.

6. **Exponentiation (^):** To raise a number to a power, use the '^' operator. For example, '2^3' calculates '2' raised to the power of '3', resulting in '8'.

6.2 Assignment Operator

The assignment operator ('<-' or '=') is used to assign values to variables. It allows you to store data for future use. For example, to store the value '10' in a variable named 'x', you can use either 'x <- 10' or 'x = 10'.

6.3   Comparison Operator

Comparison operators are essential for making logical comparisons between values:

1. **Equal (==):** The equal operator '==' checks if two values are equal. For example, '5 == 5' evaluates to 'TRUE'.

2. **Not Equal (!=):** The not equal operator '!=' checks if two values are not equal. For example, '3 != 7' evaluates to 'TRUE'.

3. **Greater Than (>):** To determine if the left operand is greater than the right operand, use the greater-than operator '>'. For instance, '8 > 4' results in 'TRUE'.

4. **Less Than (<):** The less-than operator '<' checks if the left operand is less than the right operand. For example, '2 < 9' yields 'TRUE'.

5. **Greater Than or Equal To (>=):** This operator '>=' checks if the left operand is greater than or equal to the right operand. For example, '6 >= 6' evaluates to 'TRUE'.

6. **Less Than or Equal To (<=):** The less-than-or-equal-to operator '<=' checks if the left operand is

less than or equal to the right operand. For instance, '5 <= 3' evaluates to 'FALSE'.

6.4 Logical Operator

Logical operators are used for making logical decisions and combining conditions:

1. **AND ('&'):** The AND operators combine two logical expressions and return 'TRUE' only if both expressions are 'TRUE'. For example, 'TRUE & FALSE' evaluates to 'FALSE'.

2. **OR ('|'):** The OR operators combine two logical expressions and return 'TRUE' if at least one expression is 'TRUE'. For instance, 'TRUE | FALSE' evaluates to 'TRUE'.

3. **NOT ('!'):** The NOT operator negates a logical expression. It returns 'TRUE' if the expression is 'FALSE' and vice versa. For example, '!TRUE' evaluates to 'FALSE'.

6.5 The Pipe Operator (%>%)

The pipe operator, denoted by '%>%', is a powerful tool for creating data pipelines, especially when working with the 'dplyr' package in R. This operator allows you to chain multiple operations together, applying them sequentially to a dataset. The result of one operation becomes the input for the next, streamlining your code and improving readability.

7 Basic Operations in R

Before diving into the world of statistical analysis and data modeling, it's crucial to grasp the fundamental operations in R. These basic operations form the backbone of your statistical toolkit and allow you to perform essential calculations, manipulate data, and make informed decisions. In this section, we will explore these basic operations with easy-to-follow examples related to statistics.

7.1 Arithmetic Operation

Arithmetic operations are the foundation of mathematical calculations. Here are some basic arithmetic operators and their use in statistics:

- **Addition (+):** The addition operator combines values, often used in aggregating data. For instance, calculating the sum of a dataset:

```
# Calculate the sum of a numeric vector.
data <- c(5, 8, 12, 7, 10)
sum_result <- sum(data)
sum_result

## [1] 42
```

- **Subtraction (-):** Subtraction is useful for finding differences, such as computing the change between two values:

```r
# Calculate the difference between two values.
initial_value <- 50
final_value <- 68
change <- final_value - initial_value
change
```

```
## [1] 18
```

- **Multiplication (*):** Multiplication can be employed in statistical modeling, e.g., scaling variables:

```r
# Scale a variable by multiplying.
variable <- c(3, 6, 9, 12, 15)
scaled_variable <- variable * 2
scaled_variable
```

```
## [1]  6 12 18 24 30
```

- **Division (/):** Division plays a role in calculating averages and proportions:

```r
# Calculate the average of a dataset.
data <- c(5, 8, 12, 7, 10)
average <- sum(data) / length(data)
average
```

```
## [1] 8.4
```

- **Modulus (%%):** The modulus operator calculates remainders, which can be useful for periodicity analysis:

```
# Check if a number is even.
number <- 15
is_even <- number %% 2 == 0
is_even
```

```
## [1] FALSE
```

- **Exponentiation (^):** Exponentiation is used in exponential growth models and transformations:

```
# Calculate exponential growth.
initial_value <- 100
growth_rate <- 0.05
final_value <- initial_value * (1 + growth_rate)^5
final_value
```

```
## [1] 127.6282
```

7.2   Assignment Operation

The assignment operator (<- or =) is used to store values or results in variables, crucial for working with data and statistical formulas:

```
# Store the result of a calculation in a variable.
mean_value <- mean(data)
mean_value
```

```
## [1] 8.4
```

7.3   Comparison Operation

Comparison operators are essential in statistics for making logical comparisons:

- **Equal (==):** Used for checking equality, e.g., comparing data points:

  ```
  # Check if two values are equal.
  value1 <- 8
  value2 <- 8
  are_equal <- value1 == value2
  are_equal
  ```

  ```
  ## [1] TRUE
  ```

- **Not Equal (!=):** Used to identify differences, for instance, comparing group means:

  ```
  # Check if two values are not equal.
  mean1 <- 25
  mean2 <- 30
  are_different <- mean1 != mean2
  are_different
  ```

```
## [1] TRUE
```

- **Greater Than (>):** Useful for comparing values in hypothesis testing:

```
# Check if one value is greater than another.
p_value <- 0.03
is_significant <- p_value < 0.05
is_significant
```

```
## [1] TRUE
```

- **Less Than (<):** Employed in statistical modeling for model selection:

```
# Compare two model fits.
AIC_model1 <- 120
AIC_model2 <- 110
is_better_model <- AIC_model1 < AIC_model2
is_better_model
```

```
## [1] FALSE
```

- **Greater Than or Equal To (>=):** Frequently used when setting decision boundaries:

```
# Determine if a value is greater than or equal to a
threshold.
threshold <- 0.05
```

```r
is_acceptable <- p_value >= threshold
is_acceptable
```

```
## [1] FALSE
```

- **Less Than or Equal To (<=):** Important for defining cutoff values in statistics:

```r
# Check if a value is less than or equal to a critical
point.
critical_value <- 1.96
z_score <- 2.37
is_critical <- z_score <= critical_value
is_critical
```

```
## [1] FALSE
```

7.4 Logical Operation

Logical operators are essential for making logical decisions and combining conditions in statistics:

- **AND (&):** Used to ensure that multiple conditions are met simultaneously:

```r
# Combine two conditions using AND.
condition1 <- TRUE
condition2 <- FALSE
is_met <- condition1 & condition2
is_met
```

```
## [1] FALSE
```

- **OR (|):** Employed when either of multiple conditions can be true:

```
# Combine two conditions using OR.
condition1 <- TRUE
condition2 <- FALSE
is_met <- condition1 | condition2
is_met

## [1] TRUE
```

- **NOT (!):** Used to negate a condition or make an opposite statement:

```
# Negate a condition using NOT.
condition <- TRUE
is_not_met <- !condition
is_not_met

## [1] FALSE
```

These basic operations lay the groundwork for your statistical journey with R. In the upcoming sections, we'll apply these operations in real-world statistical analyses, from data manipulation to hypothesis testing and model building.

8   Variable Naming in R

In the world of data analysis and statistics, one of the fundamental aspects of programming in R is the proper naming of variables. In this section, we will delve into the art and science of variable naming in R, covering best practices, conventions, and strategies for creating informative and manageable variable names.

8.1   Why Variable Naming Matters

Understanding why variable naming is crucial for code readability, maintainability, and collaboration. We'll discuss the impact of well-named variables on the entire data analysis process. Explore common mistakes and pitfalls in variable naming that can lead to confusion and errors. Learn how to avoid these issues in your own code.

8.2   Rules for Naming Variables

Discuss the basic rules and guidelines for naming variables in R, including:

1   **Start with a Letter:** Variable names must start with a letter. They cannot start with a number. We'll explore how this rule ensures valid variable names.

2   **No Spaces Allowed:** Spaces are not allowed in variable names. We'll discuss the importance of using

underscores or periods to separate words in variable names.

3 **Avoiding Keywords:** R has reserved keywords that cannot be used as variable names. We'll provide a list of these keywords and explain how to avoid conflicts.

4 **Alphanumeric Characters Only:** Variable names should consist of alphanumeric characters (letters and numbers) and underscores or periods. Special characters like % and $ cannot be used in variable names.

8.3   Norms of Naming Variables

- **Naming Conventions:** Introduce naming conventions and standards commonly followed in the R community, considering the rules mentioned above. We'll discuss conventions for different types of variables, including functions, constants, and data structures.

- **Choosing Descriptive Names:** Explore strategies for selecting descriptive and meaningful variable names. Learn how to strike the right balance between clarity and brevity while adhering to the naming rules.

8.4 Creating Informative Variable Names

Walk through practical examples of creating clear and informative variable names for data frames, vectors, and functions.

```r
# Example: Creating informative variable names
employee_data <- data.frame(
  emp_id = 1:3,
  emp_name = c("Afzal", "Sifat", "Sumon"),
  emp_salary = c(50000, 60000, 55000)
)
employee_data

##   emp_id emp_name emp_salary
## 1      1    Afzal      50000
## 2      2    Sifat      60000
## 3      3    Sumon      55000
```

8.5 Avoiding Ambiguity

Discuss strategies for avoiding ambiguity in variable names while adhering to the rules. We'll cover how to differentiate variables with similar meanings and handle different contexts.

```r
# Example: Avoiding ambiguity in variable names
temp_mean <- c(25, 28, 30, 22, 27)
rainfall_mean <- c(0, 5, 2, 10, 3)
```

8.6   Variable Naming for Data Analysis

Explore techniques for naming variables in the context of data analysis and statistics while maintaining the naming rules. Discuss how to name variables related to statistical tests, modeling, and visualization.

8.7   Self-documenting Code

Learn how well-named variables can serve as documentation for your code, emphasizing clarity and adherence to the naming rules. Discover how self-documenting code makes your work more understandable and accessible to others.

In this section, we've uncovered the essential aspects of variable naming in R while adhering to the fundamental rules. You've learned the significance of choosing descriptive and meaningful variable names, adhering to naming conventions, and avoiding common pitfalls. With this knowledge, you'll be better equipped to write clear, readable, and maintainable R code, making your data analysis tasks more efficient and effective.

9   R Data Objects & Statistical Operations

In R, data objects are the building blocks for data analysis and statistical operations. Understanding the different data types and how to manipulate them is crucial for effective data analysis. This section explores the primary data objects in R and demonstrates statistical operations, data manipulation, and matrix operations using practical examples.

9.1   R Data Objects

9.1.1   Vectors

Vectors are one-dimensional data objects in R. They can hold elements of the same data type, such as numeric, character, or logical values. Vectors are fundamental for storing and analyzing data.

```r
# Creating a numeric vector
numeric_vector <- c(1, 2, 3, 4, 5)
numeric_vector
```

```
## [1] 1 2 3 4 5
```

```r
# Creating a character vector
character_vector <- c("Data", "Info", "Knowledge")
character_vector
```

```
## [1] "Data"  "Info"    "Knowledge"
```

```r
# Creating a logical vector
logical_vector <- c(TRUE, FALSE, TRUE)
logical_vector
```

```
## [1]  TRUE FALSE  TRUE
```

9.1.2 Matrices & Arrays

Matrices and arrays are multi-dimensional data objects. Matrices have two dimensions, while arrays can have more than two. They are used for organizing data in rows and columns or higher dimensions.

```r
# Creating a matrix
matrix_data <- matrix(data = c(1, 2, 3, 4, 5, 6), nrow = 2,
ncol = 3)
matrix_data

##      [,1] [,2] [,3]
## [1,]   1    3    5
## [2,]   2    4    6

# Creating an array
array_data <- array(data = c(1, 2, 3, 4, 5, 6), dim = c(2, 3,
1))
array_data

## , , 1
##
##      [,1] [,2] [,3]
## [1,]   1    3    5
## [2,]   2    4    6
```

9.1.3 Data Frames

Data frames are tabular data structures that can hold data of different data types in columns. They are commonly used for organizing and analyzing datasets.

```r
# Creating a data frame
data_frame <- data.frame(Name = c("Afzal", "Sifat", "Sumon"),
                Age = c(25, 30, 22),
                Score = c(95, 88, 73))
data_frame

##      Name Age Score
## 1  Afzal  25    95
## 2  Sifat  30    88
## 3  Sumon  22    73
```

9.1.4 Lists

Lists are versatile data objects that can hold elements of different data types. They are useful for storing diverse information or data structures.

```r
# Creating a list
my_list <- list("Joy", 28, c(85, 90, 75))
my_list

## [[1]]
## [1] "Joy"
```

```
##
## [[2]]
## [1] 28
##
## [[3]]
## [1] 85 90 75
```

In R, lists are versatile data structures that allow you to store various types of data, including vectors, matrices, and other lists. When working with lists, you may encounter a common question: What is the difference between using one set of square brackets [ ] and two sets of square brackets [[ ]] to access and manipulate list elements? Let's explore this difference and understand when to use each of these notations.

9.1.4.1 Using One Set of Square Brackets [ ]

One set of square brackets [ ] is used to extract a sublist from a list. This notation allows you to create a new list containing a subset of elements from the original list.

```
# Example 1: Using [ ] to extract a sublist
my_list <- list(apples = 5, bananas = 7, oranges = 3)
subset_list <- my_list[c("apples", "bananas")]
subset_list

## $apples
## [1] 5
```

```
## 
## $bananas
## [1] 7
```

In this example, subset_list contains a sublist of my_list with only the elements "apples" and "bananas." The result is a new list.

9.1.4.2 Using Two Sets of Square Brackets [[ ]]

Two sets of square brackets [[ ]] are used to extract a single element from a list. This notation directly retrieves the specified element and not a sublist.

```
# Example 2: Using [[ ]] to extract a single element
my_list <- list(apples = 5, bananas = 7, oranges = 3)
num_apples <- my_list[["apples"]]
num_apples
```

```
## [1] 5
```

In this example, num_apples contains the value 5, which is the value associated with the "apples" element in my_list.

9.1.4.3 When to Use Each Notation

The choice between [ ] and [[ ]] depends on your specific task:

- **Use [ ]** when you want to extract a subset of elements from a list, creating a new list with those elements. This is useful for creating sublists or working with multiple elements simultaneously.

- **Use [[ ]]** when you want to access a single element from a list. This is typically used when you need the actual value associated with that element.

9.1.4.4 Additional Considerations

When using [[ ]], you provide the specific name or index of the element you want to access. With [ ], you can use vectors or logical conditions to select multiple elements, providing greater flexibility for subsetting lists.

Understanding the distinction between one set of square brackets and two sets of square brackets is essential for effective list manipulation in R. By choosing the appropriate notation, you can efficiently work with your data and create more readable and concise code.

In the following sections, we will explore more advanced list operations and practical examples that demonstrate the power of lists in R.

9.1.5 Factors

Factors are used to represent categorical data. They are particularly useful in statistical modeling and data analysis.

```r
# Creating a factor
gender <- factor(c("Male", "Female", "Male", "Male"),
levels = c('Male', 'Female'))
gender

## [1] Male   Female Male   Male
## Levels: Male Female
```

9.2 Matrix Operations

This section focuses on matrix operations and their practical applications in solving real-world problems, specifically in the context of stochastic processes. We will cover various matrix operations, from basic concepts to advanced applications.

9.2.1 Matrix Multiplication

Matrix multiplication is fundamental for various applications, from linear transformations to solving systems of linear equations. We'll explore how to perform matrix multiplication in R.

```r
# Example: Matrix multiplication
A <- matrix(c(1, 2, 3, 4), nrow = 2)
```

```r
B <- matrix(c(2, 0, 1, 3), nrow = 2)
result <- A %*% B
result
```

```
##      [,1] [,2]
## [1,]   2   10
## [2,]   4   14
```

9.2.2 Matrix Inverse

Matrix inversion is essential for solving linear systems and has applications in statistics and data analysis. We'll discuss how to find the inverse of a matrix.

```r
# Example: Matrix inversion
A <- matrix(c(1, 0, 2, 4), nrow = 2)
solve(A)
```

```
##      [,1] [,2]
## [1,]    1 -0.50
## [2,]    0  0.25
```

9.2.3 Matrix Transpose

Matrix transposition is a simple yet important operation for changing the orientation of a matrix. We'll show how to perform matrix transposition.

```r
# Example: Matrix transpose
A <- matrix(c(1, 2, 3, 4), nrow = 2)
t(A)
```

```
##      [,1] [,2]
## [1,]   1    2
## [2,]   3    4
```

9.2.4 Naming Rows & Columns

Assigning meaningful names to rows and columns enhances data interpretation. We'll illustrate how to name rows and columns in a matrix.

```r
# Example: Naming rows and columns
A <- matrix(1:6, nrow = 2)
rownames(A) <- c("Row1", "Row2")
colnames(A) <- c("Column1", "Column2", "Column3")
A
```

```
##      Column1 Column2 Column3
## Row1    1       3       5
## Row2    2       4       6
```

9.2.5 Slicing and Partitioning

Matrix slicing allows you to extract specific elements or submatrices. We'll demonstrate how to slice matrices in R.

```
# Example: Matrix slicing
A <- matrix(1:9, nrow = 3)
submatrix <- A[1:2, 2:3]
submatrix
```

```
##      [,1] [,2]
## [1,]   4   7
## [2,]   5   8
```

9.2.6 Vectorization

Vectorization simplifies matrix operations by applying functions to entire vectors. We'll explore the concept of vectorization and its advantages.

```
# Example: Vectorization
A <- matrix(1:9, nrow = 3)
colSums(A)
```

```
## [1] 6 15 24
```

9.2.7 Kronecker Product

The Kronecker product is used for combining matrices. We'll demonstrate how to compute the Kronecker product of two matrices.

```
# Example: Kronecker product
A <- matrix(1:4, nrow = 2)
```

```r
B <- matrix(0:1, nrow = 2)
kronecker(A, B)
```

```
##      [,1] [,2]
## [1,]   0   0
## [2,]   1   3
## [3,]   0   0
## [4,]   2   4
```

9.2.8 Scalar Multiplication & Orthogonal Matrices

Scalar multiplication and orthogonal matrices play a significant role in linear transformations and eigenvalue problems. We'll discuss these concepts with examples.

```r
# Example: Scalar multiplication and orthogonal
matrices
A <- matrix(1:4, nrow = 2)
scalar_multiplied <- A * 2
orthogonal_matrix <- qr.Q(qr(A))
orthogonal_matrix
```

```
##           [,1]       [,2]
## [1,] -0.4472136 -0.8944272
## [2,] -0.8944272  0.4472136
```

This section provides a comprehensive understanding of matrix operations. By mastering these concepts, you'll be well-equipped for advanced statistical analysis.

9.2.9 Eigenvalues & Eigenvectors

Eigenvalues and eigenvectors are fundamental concepts in linear algebra and have numerous applications in statistics, data analysis, and machine learning. In this section, we will explore how to compute and utilize eigenvalues and eigenvectors of a matrix in R.

9.2.9.1 Eigenvalues & Eigenvectors: An Overview

Eigenvalues and eigenvectors are properties of square matrices. Given a square matrix A, an eigenvalue (λ) and its corresponding eigenvector (v) satisfy the equation:

$$A \cdot v = \lambda \cdot v$$

- An eigenvalue represents a scalar that scales the eigenvector.

- An eigenvector is a non-zero vector that remains in the same direction after the matrix transformation.

9.2.9.2 Computing Eigenvalues and Eigenvectors in R

In R, you can compute the eigenvalues and eigenvectors of a matrix using the eigen() function. Here's how you can do it:

```r
# Create a matrix
A <- matrix(c(3, -1, 2, 4), nrow = 2)
# Compute eigenvalues and eigenvectors
eigen_result <- eigen(A)
round(eigen_result$values, 2)

## [1] 3.5+1.32i 3.5-1.32i

round(eigen_result$vectors, 2)

##          [,1]      [,2]
## [1,] 0.82+0.00i 0.82+0.00i
## [2,] 0.20+0.54i 0.20-0.54i
```

In the above code, we create a 2×2 matrix 'A' and use the eigen() function to compute its eigenvalues and eigenvectors. The result is stored in 'eigen_result', from which we extract the eigenvalues and eigenvectors.

9.3   Data Frame Operations in R

9.3.1   Slicing a Data Frame

Slicing a data frame is a fundamental operation in R when you need to select specific rows and columns of the data for further analysis or manipulation. In this section, we'll explore various methods for slicing data frames, including subsetting rows and columns using indexing.

9.3.1.1   Basic Slicing

The basic way to slice a data frame in R is by using square brackets [ ]. You can specify which rows and columns you want to select using indexing. Here's how it works:

```r
# Create a sample data frame
my_data <- data.frame(
  Name = c("Afzal", "Sifat", "Sumon", "Tonmoy"),
  Age = c(25, 30, 22, 28),
  Salary = c(50000, 60000, 55000, 62000)
)
# Slice rows 2 and 3, and columns 1 and 2
my_data[2:3, 1:2]

##    Name Age
## 2 Sifat  30
## 3 Sumon  22
```

In this example, subset_data contains rows 2 and 3 of the data frame and columns 1 and 2. The result is a new data frame with the selected subset.

9.3.1.2 Negative Indexing

You can also use negative indexing to exclude specific rows or columns. For example, if you want to exclude the third row and the last column, you can do the following:

```
# Exclude row 3 and the last column
my_data[-3, -ncol(my_data)]

##    Name Age
## 1 Afzal  25
## 2 Sifat  30
## 4 Tonmoy  28
```

The ncol(data) function is used to determine the number of columns in the data frame.

9.3.1.3 Named Indexing

If your data frame has named columns, you can use names to select specific columns. For instance, if you want to select only the "Name" and "Salary" columns, you can do the following:

```
# Select specific columns by name
my_data[, c("Name", "Salary")]
```

```
##    Name Salary
## 1 Afzal 50000
## 2 Sifat 60000
## 3 Sumon 55000
## 4 Tonmoy 62000
```

This method is useful when your data frame has many columns, and you only want to work with a few of them.

9.3.1.4 Logical Indexing

You can also use logical indexing to subset rows based on conditions. For example, if you want to select rows where the age is greater than 25:

```
# Select rows based on a condition
my_data[my_data$Age > 25, ]
```

```
##    Name Age Salary
## 2 Sifat 30 60000
## 4 Tonmoy 28 62000
```

This creates a new data frame containing only the rows that meet the specified condition.

9.3.2 Advanced Slicing

R offers more advanced slicing options, such as using the dplyr package for data manipulation or selecting specific columns based on patterns in their names. These methods can be particularly useful for complex data manipulation tasks. The dplyr package is a powerful tool for data manipulation and transformation. It offers a concise and intuitive way to slice, filter, and arrange data frames. In this section, we will explore advanced slicing techniques using dplyr functions, and we'll leverage the pipeline operator (%>%) for a streamlined workflow.

9.3.2.1 Selecting Columns with select()

The select() function allows you to choose specific columns of interest in a data frame. It's especially handy when you have a data frame with many columns, and you only want to work with a subset of them.

```r
library(dplyr) # Loading library

# Select columns "Name" and "Salary"
selected_data <- my_data %>%
  select(Name, Salary)
selected_data
```

```
##    Name Salary
## 1 Afzal 50000
## 2 Sifat 60000
## 3 Sumon 55000
## 4 Tonmoy 62000
```

Using the %>% operator, we can pass the data frame to the select() function, specifying the columns we want to retain.

9.3.2.2 Filtering Rows with filter()

The filter() function helps you filter rows based on specific conditions. This is a versatile tool for creating subsets of data based on your criteria.

```r
# Filter rows where "Age" is greater than 25
filtered_data <- my_data %>%
  filter(Age > 25)
filtered_data
```

```
##    Name Age Salary
## 1 Sifat  30  60000
## 2 Tonmoy 28  62000
```

By chaining %>%, you can easily create a filtered data frame where only rows meeting your condition are retained.

9.3.2.3 Arranging Data with arrange()

arrange() is used to reorder rows based on one or more columns. This is particularly useful when you want to sort your data by specific variables.

```r
# Arrange data by ascending "Salary" and descending
"Age"
arranged_data <- my_data %>%
  arrange(Salary, desc(Age))
arranged_data

##    Name Age Salary
## 1 Afzal  25  50000
## 2 Sumon  22  55000
## 3 Sifat  30  60000
## 4 Tonmoy 28  62000
```

In this example, we arrange the data frame first by ascending "Salary" and then by descending "Age."

9.3.2.4 Combining select, filter, and arrange

One of the strengths of dplyr is the ability to chain multiple operations together using the pipeline operator, %>%. This creates a clear and concise data manipulation workflow.

```r
# Select specific columns, filter rows, and arrange the
data
result <- my_data %>%
  select(Name, Age, Salary) %>%
  filter(Age > 25) %>%
  arrange(Salary)
result
```

```
##    Name Age Salary
## 1 Sifat 30 60000
## 2 Tonmoy 28 62000
```

This code first selects specific columns, then filters rows based on an age condition, and finally arranges the data by salary.

9.3.2.5 Additional dplyr Functions

Beyond select, filter, and arrange, the dplyr package offers other useful functions like mutate for creating new variables, group_by for grouping data, and summarize for generating summary statistics.

In this section, we've covered the basics of slicing data frames in R. You've learned how to select specific rows and columns using indexing, exclude rows and columns using negative indexing, and work with named and logical indexing. The ability to slice data frames effectively is essential for data analysis and manipulation tasks.

9.4 Statistical Operations

9.4.1 Descriptive Statistics

You can perform descriptive statistics on vectors, data frames, and other data objects. Common functions include mean(), median(), sd(), and summary().

```r
# Calculate mean and median
mean(data_frame$Score)

## [1] 85.33333

median(data_frame$Age)

## [1] 25

# Summary statistics
summary(data_frame)

##     Name                Age           Score
## Length:3           Min.  :22.00  Min.  :73.00
## Class :character   1st Qu.:23.50  1st Qu.:80.50
## Mode  :character   Median :25.00  Median :88.00
##                    Mean  :25.67  Mean  :85.33
##                    3rd Qu.:27.50  3rd Qu.:91.50
##                    Max.  :30.00  Max.  :95.00
```

10 Conditional Structures

Conditional structures in R allow you to make decisions based on conditions. The most common conditional structure is the if statement. Here's a simple example of how to use conditional structures in R:

```r
# Sample data
x <- 10
```

```r
# Simple if statement
if (x > 5) {
  cat("x is greater than 5\n")
} else {
  cat("x is not greater than 5\n")
}

## x is greater than 5
```

In this example, we have a variable x with the value 10. We use an if statement to check if x is greater than 5. If the condition is true, the code inside the first block is executed, which in this case, prints "x is greater than 5." If the condition is false, the code inside the else block is executed, which prints "x is not greater than 5."

You can also use else if to specify multiple conditions:

```r
# Sample data
x <- 7
```

```r
# Multiple conditions with if-else if-else
if (x < 5) {
  cat("x is less than 5\n")
} else if (x == 5) {
  cat("x is equal to 5\n")
} else {
```

```r
  cat("x is greater than 5\n")
}
```

x is greater than 5

In this example, we check if x is less than 5, equal to 5, or greater than 5 and print a corresponding message.

R also supports the switch function for multi-case conditions:

```r
# Sample data
day <- "Monday"

# Using switch function
message <- switch(day,
  "Monday" = "It's the start of the week.",
  "Tuesday" = "It's Tuesday.",
  "Wednesday" = "It's the middle of the week.",
  "Thursday" = "It's almost Friday.",
  "Friday" = "It's the end of the week.",
  "Saturday" = "It's the weekend.",
  "Sunday" = "It's still the weekend."
)


cat(message, "\n")
```

It's the start of the week.

In this example, the switch function is used to assign different messages based on the value of the day variable.

The ifelse function in R is a powerful tool for vectorized conditional statements. It allows you to perform element-wise conditional evaluations on vectors or data frames and return a new vector based on the conditions specified.

The basic syntax of the ifelse function is as follows:

ifelse(test, yes, no)

- **test:** The condition to be evaluated. It can be a logical vector, a comparison, or any expression that results in a logical vector.

- **yes:** The value to be returned when the condition is TRUE.

- **no:** The value to be returned when the condition is FALSE.

Here's an example of how to use ifelse:

```r
# Create a vector of ages
ages <- c(25, 42, 18, 31, 57, 22)
# Use ifelse to categorize ages as "Young" or "Adult"
age_category <- ifelse(ages < 30, "Young", "Adult")
print(age_category)
```

```
## [1] "Young" "Adult" "Young" "Adult" "Adult" "Young"
```

In this example, we create a vector of ages and use ifelse to categorize them as "Young" if they are less than 30 and "Adult" otherwise. The result will be a new vector, age_category, with the corresponding categories.

You can use ifelse in more complex scenarios and with different data types. It's a versatile function for creating conditional logic in R.

Here's an example of using ifelse to create a new variable in a data frame:

```r
# Create a data frame
score_data <- data.frame(Name = c("Afzal", "Sifat",
"Sumon", "Tonmoy"),
          Score = c(85, 62, 47, 73))
# Use ifelse to create a new variable "Status"
score_data $Status <- ifelse(score_data $Score >= 60,
"Pass", "Fail")
score_data
```

```
##     Name Score Status
## 1  Afzal    85  Pass
## 2  Sifat    62  Pass
## 3  Sumon    47  Fail
## 4 Tonmoy    73  Pass
```

In this example, we use ifelse to create a new variable "Status" based on the "Score" column. If the score is greater than or equal to 60, it's labeled as "Pass"; otherwise, it's labeled as "Fail."

ifelse is particularly handy when you need to perform conditional operations on vectors or data frames, making your code more concise and efficient.

These are basic examples of conditional structures in R. You can use more complex conditions and combine multiple conditions using logical operators (& for "and," | for "or," ! for "not") to control the flow of your R code based on specific criteria.

11   Looping in R for Statistical Analysis

Loops are fundamental constructs in programming that allow you to execute a block of code repeatedly. In R, loops are particularly valuable when you need to perform operations on multiple elements within a data structure, or when you want to automate repetitive tasks. This section explores the different types of loops in R and provides practical examples of their application in statistical analysis.

11.1 Types of Loops

11.1.1 For Loop

The for loop in R is used to iterate over a sequence, such as a vector or a sequence of numbers. It repeatedly executes a set of statements for each element in the sequence. Here's a basic example:

```r
# Simple for loop to print numbers from 1 to 5
for (i in 1:5) {
  print(i)
}

## [1] 1
## [1] 2
## [1] 3
## [1] 4
## [1] 5
```

11.1.2 While Loop

The while loop in R repeatedly executes a block of code as long as a specified condition is true. It's useful when the number of iterations is not known in advance. Here's a simple example:

```r
# While loop to print numbers from 1 to 5
i <- 1
while (i <= 5) {
```

```
 print(i)
 i <- i + 1
}
```

```
## [1] 1
## [1] 2
## [1] 3
## [1] 4
## [1] 5
```

11.1.3 Repeat Loop

The repeat loop is a simple, infinite loop in R that continues executing until explicitly stopped. It's not commonly used, but can be helpful in specific scenarios. You need to include a condition to break the loop manually.

```
# Repeat loop with a break statement
i <- 1
repeat {
 print(i)
 i <- i + 1
 if (i > 5) {
   break
 }
}
```

```
## [1] 1
## [1] 2
```

```
## [1] 3
## [1] 4
## [1] 5
```

11.1.4 Apply Functions

R offers functions like lapply, sapply, and apply that allow you to apply a given function to elements of a list or matrix. These functions are often more efficient and concise than writing explicit loops.

```r
# Using lapply to apply a function to a list
numbers <- list(1, 2, 3, 4, 5)

squared <- lapply(numbers, function(x) x^2)
squared
```

```
## [[1]]
## [1] 1
##
## [[2]]
## [1] 4
##
## [[3]]
## [1] 9
##
## [[4]]
## [1] 16
##
```

```
## [[5]]
## [1] 25
```

11.2 Practical Applications

11.2.1 Data Cleaning & Transformation

Loops can be used to iterate over rows or columns in a dataset, making it easy to perform data cleaning and transformation tasks.

```
my_data <- data.frame(x = sample(1:30, 5), y = sample(1:30, 5))
```

```
# Loop to standardize numeric columns in a data frame
for (col in names(my_data)) {
 if (is.numeric(my_data[[col]])) {
  my_data[[col]] <- (my_data[[col]] -
mean(my_data[[col]])) / sd(my_data[[col]])
 }
}
my_data
```

```
##         x         y
## 1 -0.4764735  0.6200532
## 2 -1.4974882 -0.6952112
## 3  0.6579873  1.4655804
## 4  0.9983255 -0.6012637
## 5  0.3176490 -0.7891587
```

11.2.2 Central Limit Theorem (CLT)

CLT is a useful technique used in statistics. Loops can help generate multiple samples and calculate averages on each.

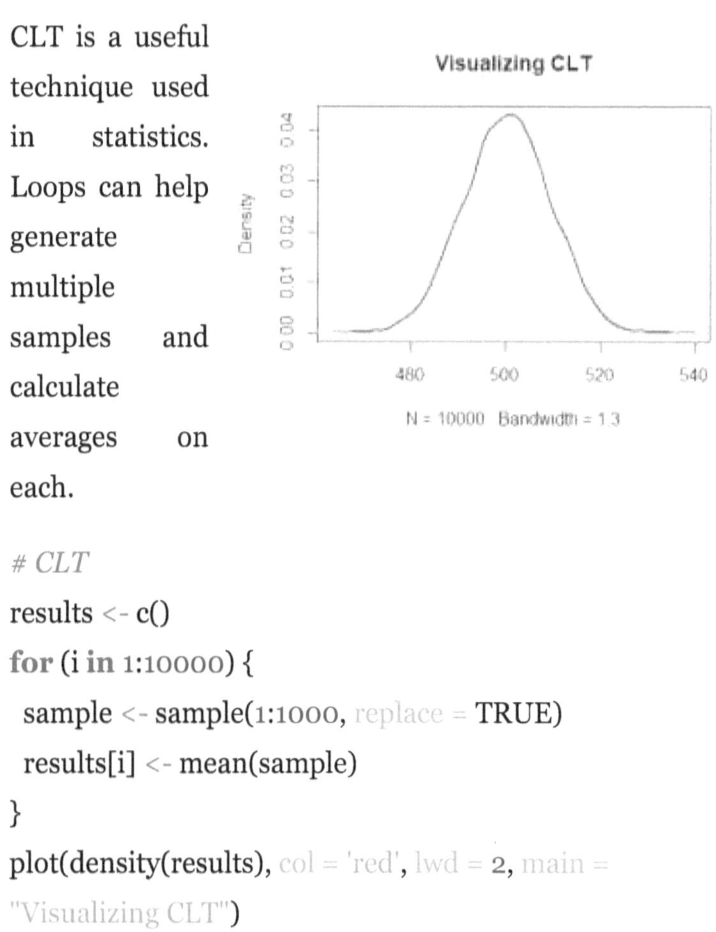


```
# CLT
results <- c()
for (i in 1:10000) {
  sample <- sample(1:1000, replace = TRUE)
  results[i] <- mean(sample)
}
plot(density(results), col = 'red', lwd = 2, main = "Visualizing CLT")
```

From the above figure we can easily understand CLT.

12 Functions in R

Functions are a fundamental concept in R, allowing you to encapsulate a series of operations into a single unit. In this section, we'll explore different types of functions, including basic functions, user-defined functions, built-in functions, and recursive functions. We'll also cover how to call these functions and provide examples to demonstrate their use.

12.1 Built-in Functions

Built-in functions are part of the R language and provide a wide range of functionalities. Here are a few examples of basic functions:

- **print()**: Used to display output.

- **sum()**: Calculates the sum of a vector of numbers.

- **mean()**: Computes the mean of a vector.

- **sqrt()**: Calculates the square root of a number.

  Example of using a basic function:

```r
# Calculate the sum of numbers
numbers <- c(1, 2, 3, 4, 5)
result <- sum(numbers)
result
```

```
## [1] 15
```

The D() function in R is part of the stats package and is used for symbolic differentiation. It takes an expression and a variable name as arguments and computes the derivative of the expression with respect to the specified variable.

```
# Define the expression
expression <- expression(x^2 + 3 * x - 2)
# Calculate the derivative
derivative <- D(expression, "x")
# Display the derivative
derivative
```

```
## 2 * x + 3
```

In this example, we use the D() function to calculate the derivative of the expression with respect to the variable "x".

12.1.1 Numerical Integration

R provides several built-in functions and packages for numerical integration. These methods are useful when you need to approximate the integral of a function over a specific interval.

The integrate() function is a versatile tool for numerical integration. It automatically selects an appropriate integration method based on the function provided.

```r
# Define a function to integrate
f <- function(x) {
  return(x^2)
}
```

```r
# Calculate the definite integral of the function over [0, 1]
result <- integrate(f, lower = 0, upper = 1)
result
```

```r
## 0.3333333 with absolute error < 3.7e-15
```

In this example, we define a function $f(x) = x^2$ and use integrate() to calculate the definite integral of f over the interval [0, 1].

The pracma package offers additional numerical integration methods. The quad() function is one such method.

```r
# Install and load the pracma package (if not already installed)
# install.packages("pracma")
library(pracma)
```

```r
# Define a function to integrate
f <- function(x) {
```

```
  return(x^3)
}
```

```
# Calculate the definite integral of the function over [0, 1]
result <- quad(f, 0, 1)
result
```

```
## [1] 0.25
```

In this example, we install and load the pracma package and use the quad() function for numerical integration.

12.2 User-defined Functions

User-defined functions allow you to create custom functions tailored to your specific needs. These functions are defined using the function() keyword.

12.2.1 Derivative Function with the Concept of Limit

Let's create a user-defined function to calculate the derivative of a function using the limit definition:

```
# User-defined derivative function
derivative <- function(f, x, h = 1e-5) {
  (f(x + h) - f(x)) / h
}
```

```r
# Define a sample function
f <- function(x) {
  return(x^2)
}
```

```r
# Calculate the derivative at x = 3
result <- derivative(f, 3)
result
```

```r
## [1] 6.00001
```

12.2.2 User-defined Integration Function

Certainly, here's an example of a simple user-defined integration function in R. This function takes a user-defined function, a lower limit, an upper limit, and the number of intervals (subdivisions) and calculates the definite integral using the trapezoidal rule.

```r
# User-defined integration function using the trapezoidal rule
custom_integrate <- function(func, lower, upper, n_intervals = 1000) {
  # Calculate the width of each interval
  interval_width <- (upper - lower) / n_intervals

  # Initialize the sum
  integral_sum <- 0
```

```r
# Perform the integration using the trapezoidal rule
for (i in 1:n_intervals) {
  x_i <- lower + (i - 1) * interval_width
  x_ip1 <- lower + i * interval_width
  integral_sum <- integral_sum + 0.5 * interval_width *
(func(x_i) + func(x_ip1))
}


  return(integral_sum)
}


# Define a function to integrate (e.g., x^2)
f_x_squared <- function(x) {
  return(x^2)
}


# Calculate the definite integral of the function over [0, 1]
using the custom function
result <- custom_integrate(f_x_squared, lower = 0, upper
= 1)


# Display the result
result

## [1] 0.3333335
```

In this example, we define the custom_integrate function, which uses the trapezoidal rule to approximate the integral of a user-defined function over a specified interval with a given number of intervals (defaulting to 1000).

12.2.3 Newton-Raphson Method in R

```r
# Define the function for which you want to find the root
f <- function(x) {
  return(21 * x^2 - 71 * x - 22)
}


# Newton-Raphson method for finding a root
newton_raphson <- function(f, initial_guess, tol = 1e-6,
max_iter = 100) {
  x <- initial_guess
  iter <- 0

  while(abs(f(x)) > tol && iter < max_iter) {
    x <- x - f(x) / derivative(f, x)
    iter <- iter + 1
  }


  if (iter >= max_iter) {
    cat("Newton-Raphson did not converge\n")
  } else {
    return(MASS::fractions(x))
  }
```

```
}
```

```
# Initial guess
initial_guess <- 3
```

```
# Find the root using the Newton-Raphson method
newton_raphson(f, initial_guess)
```

```
## [1] 11/3
```

```
# Initial guess
initial_guess <- -3
```

```
# Find the root using the Newton-Raphson method
newton_raphson(f, initial_guess)
```

```
## [1] -2/7
```

In this example:

- We define the function $f(x)$ for which we want to find a root.

- The newton_raphson function implements the Newton-Raphson method, taking the function, its derivative, an initial guess, a tolerance (tol), and a maximum number of iterations (max_iter) as parameters.

- It iteratively refines the initial guess to find a root of the function.

- The method stops when the absolute value of $f(x)$ is less than the tolerance or the maximum number of iterations is reached.

- We set an initial guess and call the newton_raphson function to find the root of the function $f(x) = 21 x^2 - 71 x - 22$. The method will print the result when a root is found or indicate if it did not converge.

12.3 Recursive Function

Recursive functions are functions that call themselves. They are particularly useful for solving problems that can be broken down into smaller, similar subproblems. A classic example of a recursive function is calculating Fibonacci numbers.

```r
# Recursive function to calculate Fibonacci numbers
fibonacci <- function(n) {
 if (n <= 1) {
  return(n)
 } else {
  return(fibonacci(n - 1) + fibonacci(n - 2))
 }
}
```

```r
# Calculate the 10th Fibonacci number
result <- fibonacci(10)
result
```

```
## [1] 55
```

12.4 Calling Functions

To use a function, you simply call it with the appropriate arguments. For user-defined functions, you provide the function name and required inputs. For built-in functions, you call them directly by name.

```r
# Call a built-in function
result <- sum(1, 2, 3)
result
```

```
## [1] 6
```

```r
# Call a user-defined function
result <- derivative(f, 3)
result
```

```
## [1] 55.00021
```

Functions are a powerful tool in R, enabling you to create reusable code and streamline your data analysis and statistical modeling tasks. Understanding the different types of functions and how to use them is essential for effective programming in R.

In the following sections, we'll explore more advanced topics related to functions and how they can be applied to solve complex problems.

13 Working with Strings in R

Strings play a fundamental role in data analysis and manipulation, especially when dealing with text data. In this section, we'll explore how to work with strings in R, including techniques for splitting and removing spaces.

13.1 Basic String Operations

R provides a wide range of functions for basic string operations. Here are some common operations you might find useful:

13.1.1 Concatenation

You can concatenate strings using the paste() or paste0() functions. For example:

```r
# Concatenating strings
string1 <- "Hello,"
string2 <- "world!"
```

```r
result <- paste(string1, string2)
result
```

```r
## [1] "Hello, world!"
```

13.1.2 Substring Extraction

To extract a portion of a string, you can use the substr() function:

```r
# Extract a substring
text <- "Data Science"
substring <- substr(text, start = 1, stop = 4)

substring
```

```r
## [1] "Data"
```

13.1.3 String Length

The nchar() function calculates the length of a string:

```r
# Calculate the length of a string
text <- "Hello, world!"
length <- nchar(text)
```

```r
## [1] 13
```

13.2 Splitting Strings

13.2.1 Splitting by Delimiter

You can split a string into substrings using a specified delimiter. The strsplit() function is useful for this task:

```r
# Split a string by a delimiter
text <- "apple,banana,cherry"
split_text <- unlist(strsplit(text, ","))

split_text

## [1] "apple" "banana" "cherry"
```

13.2.2 Splitting by Space

To split a string into words based on spaces, you can use the strsplit() function with a space as the delimiter:

```r
# Split a string into words
sentence <- "This is a sample sentence"
words <- unlist(strsplit(sentence, " "))

words

## [1] "This"   "is"     "a"      "sample" "sentence"
```

13.3 Removing Spaces

Trimming spaces from the beginning and end of a string can be achieved with the trimws() function:

```r
# Remove leading and trailing spaces
text <- "  Remove spaces  "
trimmed_text <- trimws(text)

trimmed_text

## [1] "Remove spaces"
```

13.4 Pattern Matching

R provides powerful tools for pattern matching within strings. You can use functions like grep(), grepl(), and regular expressions to find and manipulate substrings based on patterns.

13.4.1 Extract Email Addresses

```r
# Extract email addresses from a text
text <- "Contact us at contact@example.com or info@domain.com for inquiries."
pattern <- "[A-Za-z0-9._%+-]+@[A-Za-z0-9.-]+\\.[A-Za-z]{2,4}"
emails <- regmatches(text, regexpr(pattern, text, perl = TRUE))

emails

## [1] "contact@example.com"
```

13.5 String Modification

You can modify strings using functions like sub() and gsub() to find and replace substrings based on patterns.

```
# Replace text in a string
text <- "This is a simple example."
new_text <- gsub("simple", "great", text)

new_text

## [1] "This is a great example."
```

13.6 String Handling Packages

In addition to base R, you can explore packages like stringr and stringi, which offer more advanced and efficient string manipulation capabilities. In the upcoming sections, we'll delve deeper into these string operations and explore more advanced techniques for working with text data in R.

14 Reading & Writing Files in R

Data is the lifeblood of statistical analysis, and in the realm of statistics, you often need to work with data from various sources and in different formats. R, a versatile tool for statistical computing, provides a range of functions and packages to read and write data in diverse file formats. In this section, we will explore the fundamental methods for reading and writing data files, with a strong focus on the statistical perspective.

14.1 Reading Data Files

14.1.1 Reading CSV Files

CSV files are a universal format for data storage, enabling easy data sharing across platforms. In R, the read.csv() function is the go-to tool for reading CSV files, making it a crucial step for statistical analysis. For example:

```
# Load a CSV file
data <- read.csv("data.csv")
```

14.1.2 Reading Excel Files

Excel files are a common data source in various domains, including business and research. R provides the readxl and openxlsx packages to read data from Excel spreadsheets. You can import Excel data for statistical analysis. For example:

```
# Install and load the readxl package
install.packages("readxl")
library(readxl)
```

```
# Load an Excel file
data <- read_excel("data.xlsx", sheet = "Sheet1")
```

14.1.3 Reading SPSS Data Files

In the field of statistics, SPSS files are often encountered. You can use the haven package to read SPSS data files in R, enabling you to analyze and model data from this format. For example:

```r
# Install and load the haven package
install.packages("haven")
library(haven)


# Load an SPSS data file
data <- read_sav("data.sav")
```

14.1.4 Reading STATA Data Files

STATA is a widely used software for data analysis. The haven package also supports reading STATA data files in R, making it seamless to access data from this source. For example:

```r
# Load a STATA data file
data <- read_dta("data.dta")
```

14.2 Writing Data Files

14.2.1 Writing CSV Files

After conducting statistical analysis, you may wish to export your results for reporting or sharing. The write.csv()

function allows you to save data frames as CSV files. For example:

```r
# Save a data frame as a CSV file
write.csv(data, "results.csv", row.names = FALSE)
```

14.2.2 Writing Excel Files

Excel remains a popular choice for data presentation and reporting. R supports writing data frames to Excel files using packages like writexl and openxlsx. For example:

```r
# Install and load the writexl package
install.packages("writexl")
library(writexl)
```

```r
# Save a data frame to an Excel file
write_xlsx(data, path = "results.xlsx")
```

14.2.3 Writing Data to SPSS

You may need to export your results back to an SPSS file for further use or reporting. The haven package, which helps with reading SPSS data, also provides the ability to write data frames to SPSS format. For example:

```r
# Save a data frame to an SPSS data file
write_sav(data, "results.sav")
```

14.2.4 Writing Data to STATA

STATA files are essential in certain research fields. The haven package facilitates writing data frames to STATA data files in R. For example:

```
# Save a data frame to a STATA data file
write_dta(data, "results.dta")
```

In the realm of statistical analysis, your ability to read and write data in various formats is essential. This section has equipped you with the knowledge and tools to handle CSV, Excel, SPSS, and STATA files, enabling you to perform data analysis, draw statistical insights, and communicate your results effectively. As a statistician, your proficiency in data file handling is a fundamental skill for making data-driven decisions.

In the following sections of this book, we will delve into specific statistical techniques and applications, building on the data manipulation and import/export skills you've acquired in this section.

15 Measures of Central Tendency Using R

In the world of statistics, measures of central tendency are fundamental tools for understanding the central or typical values within a dataset. These measures provide insights into the "center" of the data distribution, helping statisticians and data analysts to describe and summarize data. In this section, we will explore a range of key measures of central tendency and learn how to compute them using R. We will illustrate these concepts with built-in R datasets, highlighting the versatility and applicability of these measures.

15.1 AM

The AM, often referred to as the average, is a commonly used measure of central tendency. It represents the sum of all values in a dataset divided by the number of values. The AM is particularly useful for symmetric datasets. Let's calculate the AM using the mtcars dataset as an example:

```r
# Calculate the AM of the 'mpg' variable in the mtcars dataset
am_mpg <- mean(mtcars$mpg)
am_mpg
```

```
## [1] 20.09062
```

15.2 HM

The HM is relevant in situations involving rates, such as speed or efficiency calculations. It is ideal when dealing with scenarios where fluctuations affect the overall rate inversely. Let's calculate the HM using the mtcars dataset:

 # Calculate the HM of the 'mpg' variable in the mtcars dataset

```r
hm_mpg <- length(mtcars$mpg) / sum(1 / mtcars$mpg)
hm_mpg
```

```
## [1] 18.44092
```

15.3 GM

The GM is particularly useful when dealing with data that exhibits exponential growth or decay. It is well-suited for scenarios where fluctuations are proportional, such as investment returns over multiple years. Let's calculate the GM using the Iris dataset:

 # Calculate the GM of the 'Petal.Length' variable in the Iris dataset

```r
gm_petal_length <- exp(mean(log(iris$Petal.Length)))
gm_petal_length
```

```
## [1] 3.238267
```

15.4 Mode

The Mode represents the most frequently occurring value in a dataset. R doesn't have a built-in function for calculating the mode, but you can create a custom function to find it. Let's calculate the Mode using the mtcars dataset:

```r
# Custom function to calculate the Mode
calculate_mode <- function(x) {
  uniq_x <- unique(x)
  uniq_x[which.max(tabulate(match(x, uniq_x)))]
}
```

```r
# Calculate the Mode of the 'cyl' variable in the mtcars
dataset
mode_cyl <- calculate_mode(mtcars$cyl)
mode_cyl
```

```
## [1] 8
```

15.5 Median

The Median is the middle value in a dataset when it's sorted. If the dataset has an even number of values, the Median is the average of the two middle values. Let's calculate the Median using the mtcars dataset:

```r
# Calculate the Median of the 'mpg' variable in the mtcars
dataset
median_mpg <- median(mtcars$mpg)
median_mpg
```

```
## [1] 19.2
```

In the realm of statistical analysis, the choice of a measure of central tendency depends on the specific characteristics of your data and the statistical questions you aim to answer. The AM, HM, GM, Mode, and Median each have their unique applications and provide valuable insights. As a statistician, your selection of the appropriate measure is crucial for making data-driven decisions.

In the following sections of this book, we will explore advanced statistical techniques and applications, building on the foundational knowledge you've gained in this section, and demonstrating the versatility of these measures of central tendency using built-in R datasets.

16 Measures of Dispersion in Statistics Using R

In statistics, measures of dispersion help us understand the spread or variability in data. They complement measures of central tendency by providing insights into how data points are distributed around the center. In this section, we'll explore a comprehensive set of measures of dispersion, both relative and absolute, and learn how to calculate them using R. We'll use built-in R datasets to illustrate these concepts with simple code examples, along with guidance on their appropriate uses.

16.1 Absolute Measures of Dispersion

16.1.1 Range

The range is a fundamental absolute measure of dispersion. It represents the absolute difference between the maximum and minimum values in a dataset. In R, you can calculate the range using the range() function. Let's find the range of the 'mpg' variable in the mtcars dataset:

```r
# Calculate the range of the 'mpg' variable in the mtcars dataset
mpg_range <- diff(range(mtcars$mpg))
mpg_range
```

```
## [1] 23.5
```

16.1.2 Variance

Variance is another absolute measure that quantifies how individual data points deviate from the mean. It's the average of the squared differences between each data point and the mean. In R, you can calculate the variance using the var() function. Let's find the variance for the 'mpg' variable in the mtcars dataset:

```r
# Calculate the variance of the 'mpg' variable in the mtcars dataset
mpg_variance <- var(mtcars$mpg)
mpg_variance
```

```
## [1] 36.3241
```

16.1.3 Standard Deviation

The standard deviation is the square root of the variance, representing the average deviation of data points from the mean. It's another widely used absolute measure of dispersion. In R, you can calculate the standard deviation using the sd() function. Let's find the standard deviation for the 'mpg' variable:

```r
# Calculate the standard deviation of the 'mpg' variable in
the mtcars dataset
mpg_sd <- sd(mtcars$mpg)
mpg_sd
```

```
## [1] 6.026948
```

16.1.4 Mean Absolute Deviation

The Mean Absolute Deviation provides the average absolute deviation of data points from the mean. It's a measure of dispersion that's robust to outliers. Let's calculate the MAD for the 'mpg' variable:

```r
# Calculate the Mean Absolute Deviation for the 'mpg'
variable in the mtcars dataset
mpg_mean <- mean(mtcars$mpg)
mpg_mad <- mean(abs(mtcars$mpg - mpg_mean))
mpg_mad
```

[1] 4.714453

16.1.5 Median Absolute Deviation

The Median Absolute Deviation is a robust measure of dispersion that represents the median of the absolute deviations of data points from the median. It's less affected by outliers. Let's calculate the MAD for the 'mpg' variable:

```r
# Calculate the Median Absolute Deviation  for the 'mpg'
variable in the mtcars dataset
mpg_median <- median(mtcars$mpg)
mpg_mad_median <- median(abs(mtcars$mpg -
mpg_median))
mpg_mad_median
```

[1] 3.65

16.2 Relative Measures of Dispersion

16.2.1 Coefficient of Range

The coefficient of range calculates the range as a percentage of the mean, providing a relative measure of dispersion. It helps us understand the relative variability in data. Let's calculate the coefficient of range for the 'mpg' variable:

```r
# Calculate the coefficient of range for the 'mpg' variable
in the mtcars dataset
mpg_mean <- mean(mtcars$mpg)
```

```
coefficient_of_range <- (mpg_range / mpg_mean) * 100
coefficient_of_range
```

```
## [1] 116.97
```

16.2.2 Coefficient of Variation (CV)

The CV is another relative measure of dispersion and is particularly useful for comparing the relative variability of different datasets. It is calculated as the standard deviation divided by the mean, expressed as a percentage. Let's calculate the CV for the 'mpg' variable:

```
# Calculate the CV for the 'mpg' variable in the mtcars dataset
mpg_cv <- (mpg_sd / mpg_mean) * 100
mpg_cv
```

```
## [1] 29.99881
```

Measures of dispersion provide crucial insights into the variability within a dataset. In this section, we've explored both absolute and relative measures of dispersion using R, and we've used the mtcars dataset for our examples. These measures are essential tools for statistical analysis, enabling you to make informed decisions about data variability and distribution.

17 Skewness & Kurtosis

By the same way we simply calculate the skewness and kurtosis of a vector using the function skew() and kurt(). From the result of skewness and kurtosis we can draw fruitful conclusions for a numerical vector or variable.

18 What Next

Having a questioning mindset is crucial for learning advanced R programming. A learner with a curious and inquisitive approach can follow specific guidelines to enhance their R programming skills. For advancing in R, one may use advanced books on R and explore various online platforms mentioned below. Additionally, it is important to regularly practice coding, engage with the R community through forums and discussions, and work on real-world projects to apply theoretical knowledge. Leveraging resources like advanced courses, webinars, and attending workshops or conferences can also significantly contribute to mastering advanced R programming.

1. **RStudio Education:** Offers free resources and tutorials for learning R.

2. **Coursera:** Provides free access to many courses (with an option to pay for a certificate).

3. **edX:** Features free courses from institutions like Harvard and Microsoft (with an option to pay for a certificate).

4. **Swirl:** An R package that offers free, interactive R programming lessons within the R console.

5. **R-bloggers:** Aggregates free tutorials and blog posts about R.

6. **Kaggle:** Provides free courses and datasets for hands-on practice.

7. **YouTube:** Contains numerous free video tutorials on R programming.

8. **Quora:** Engage with the R programming community to get free answers and advice on various R-related topics.

9. **RPubs:** Explore free tutorials, examples, and project reports created by the R community.

10. **GitHub:** Search for repositories with R tutorials, sample code, and projects shared by the community.

11. **Stack Overflow:** Ask questions and find answers related to R programming from a large community of developers.

12. **Data Science Central:** Offers free articles, tutorials, and resources on R and data science.

13. **Reddit:** Join the r/rprogramming subreddit to discuss and find resources related to R.

14. **Google's R Style Guide:** Provides guidelines and examples for writing R code.

15. **O'Reilly Media's Free R Books:** Access free R books and resources available from O'Reilly's website.

16. **OpenIntro:** Provides free resources and textbooks that include R programming examples.

17. **Towards Data Science:** Read free articles and tutorials on R programming and data science.

18. **Medium:** Search for free articles and tutorials on R programming written by various authors.

Leveraging advanced courses, webinars, and attending workshops or conferences can also significantly contribute to mastering advanced R programming. Furthermore, incorporating AI tools such as ChatGPT, Gemini, PoeClaude, and SocraAI can provide personalized assistance, generate code snippets, debug issues, and offer advanced insights, thereby accelerating the learning process and enabling a deeper understanding of complex R programming concepts. Happy learning!

References

[1]   H. Wickham, "Hadley Wickham's Website." Accessed: Oct. 05, 2023. [Online]. Available: https://hadley.nz/.

[2]   G. James, D. Witten, T. Hastie, and R. Tibshirani, *An Introduction to Statistical Learning: with Applications in R.* Springer, 2013.

[3]   H. Wickham and G. Grolemund, *R for Data Science: Import, Tidy, Transform, Visualize, and Model Data.* O'Reilly Media, 2016.

[4]   R. Ihaka and R. Gentleman, "R: A Language for Data Analysis and Graphics," *J. Comput. Graph. Stat.*, vol. 5, no. 3, pp. 299–314, 1996, doi: 10.1080/10618600.1996.10474713.

[5]   CRAN, "The Comprehensive R Archive Network (CRAN)." 2010, Accessed: Oct. 05, 2023. [Online]. Available: http://cran.r-project.org/.

9 798227 758491